HOOKED ON
FISH ON THE GRILL

By Karen Adler, Rick Welch
and Carolyn Wells

Pig Out Publications   PO 9624   Kansas City, MO 64134

ISBN: 0-925175-19-6

Editor: Jane Doyle Guthrie
Cover and text design: Jim Langford

Printed in the United States of America

10 9 8 7 6 5 4 3 2 1 92 93 94 95 96

CONTENTS

ACKNOWLEDGMENTS

The support and enthusiasm of many have made this book a reality. Our special thanks go to Steve Znachko and Katherine Reising for the concept. The exceptional talents of Sherry Sullivan, Jo Riley, Jim Langford, and Jane Guthrie are greatly appreciated for readying this book to print. We also are indebted to Joseph Estrada, seafood manager at Meiners Sun Fresh in Kansas City, Missouri.

And for the many wonderful recipe contributions, we are grateful to the following:

Leslie Bloom, author of *Barbecue: Sizzling Fireside Know-How*

Brenda Burns, chef-owner of Californos restaurant in Kansas City, Missouri

Captain Bilbo's restaurant in Memphis, Tennessee

The Catfish Institute

Joe DiGiovanni, owner of Joe D's Wine Bar & Cafe in Kansas City, Missouri

Jack Dugan, owner of The Gentleman's Choice restaurant in San Marcos, California

Judith Fertig, author of *Kansas City Gold*

Dottie Griffith, food editor of the *Dallas Morning News* and author of *Dallas Cuisine*

Gwenn Jensen, author of *San Diego Cuisine*

The Kansas City Barbeque Society

Donnie Morris, award-winning barbecuer

New England Fisheries Development Association, Inc.

Quail's Dinnerhouse restaurant in San Marcos, California

Jim Quessenberry, award-winning barbecuer

Chris Schlesinger, Ph.B., co-author of *The Thrill of The Grill*

INTRODUCTION

Smoldering aromatic woods, fresh herb marinades, citrusy bastes and butters—these are the special elements that transform fish and seafood into the most delectable of entrees. Everything tastes better on the grill, and fish is no exception. Plus it's fast! When your cooking choice is fish on the grill, the dinner bell rings in less than an hour. And oh what you get for the effort—luscious seared shrimp, smoky curled oysters, crisp flaky fillets, or juicy fragrant steaks. In the category of just plain fun, new techniques abound for the adventurous—have you tried stir-grilling?

Obviously grilling has much to recommend it for fast-paced lifestyles, plus fresh fish and seafood are healthy, too. Fish tends to be low in fat, calories, and cholesterol and high in nutrition and protein. The wide varieties of recipes included here have been selected to tempt you, teach you, and hook you on fish on the grill. So fire up the cooker, strap on the tongs, and let your tastebuds have their way!

FISH GRILLING BASICS

When you're in the mood for a meal of fish or seafood, grilling is your quickest, easiest, and tastiest cooking option. Because fish has no tough connective tissue, it's perfect for the fast, hot nature of the grill.

Rule number one is to always use the freshest ingredients. When selecting and buying fish, go to a reputable fish and seafood market. The manager of this market, known as a *fishmonger*, will help you select the best catch of the day to throw on your grill. So be flexible—if your recipe calls for halibut but the salmon is the freshest, change your plans. The fishmonger also can suggest similar-type fish when you need to substitute, or use the "Fish Substitution Guide for the Grill" on page 12. Choose fish with bright, clear eyes, make sure the flesh is fresh and moist, and beware of an overpowering fishy odor.

Another hook to buying fish in the 1990's is farm-raised fish and seafood, a whole new safe and economical angle (pardon the puns). Farm-raised options got a boost when the federal government began regulating certain species that were overfished. For example, Gulf redfish surged in popularity during the heyday of Cajun blackened redfish recipes. Authorities banned commercial fishing of it until stocks were replenished. Now it's available again. Currently New England cod catch quotas have been cut by half, sure to affect availability and prices. So although farm-raising may seem just a forced alternative to maintaining stocks, very importantly it's raised quality and often lowered prices because of abundance of harvest. In addition, new "faces," like tilapia, are appearing on the American fish market also thanks to farm-raising.

Farm-raised catfish, a whole new taste and texture experience compared to the "wild," and tiger shrimp (farm-raised in Asia) are both plentiful, interesting choices.

Health-conscious chefs are choosing fish to grill because overall it's lower in fat and calories than other meat options. In fact, grilling itself is a very low-fat way to prepare any kind of meat. The process is as simple as seasoning the fish and lightly brushing it with a low cholesterol oil to prevent sticking. The average calorie count for an uncooked 7-ounce serving of fish ranges from 160-200 calories for haddock and catfish to 400 calories for "fatty" fish like trout and salmon.

As you begin exploring the fish and seafood recipes in this book, follow these simple preparation guidelines with each. Always rinse fish in cold water to remove any bacteria and pat it dry before marinating, seasoning, or cooking. When a recipe calls for brushing oil on the fish, make sure that you do so *lightly;* fire flare-ups can occur when oil drips on hot coals. The grill should be clean and also lightly oiled (use a long-handled brush and take care again to avoid dripping oil). Have all of your equipment handy, and your grilling experience will be relaxing and enjoyable.

For the novice fish griller, firm-fleshed fish steaks (salmon, tuna, swordfish, shark) will be the easiest to grill. They require the least amount of special equipment because their firmness allows cooking directly on the regular grill rack. They're also easier to turn. As your confidence grows, so do your food and cooking-style options. Invest in some of the new grill toppers— racks and woks—that make handling delicate foods and even stir-grilling possible on the grill. And don't forget a set of skewers; they make grilling small chunks and items like shrimp and scallops a breeze. Buy several so you can skewer vegetables on the grill, too.

The Grill

Grilling is defined as cooking over a direct heat source. The kind of grill you choose is determined by the space you have, the kind of fuel you want to use, the amount of cooking surface you need, and how much money you want to spend. The fuel choices are gas, electric, and charcoal/hardwood. Gas and electric grills are quick to start and easy to clean; their prices, of course, may be higher than a comparable-sized charcoal grill. When grilling on a gas or electric grill, follow the manufacturer's directions. Charcoal grills come in all sizes and shapes, with or without covers. The most popular grill "rig" for home use is the kettle-shaped grill. Whatever you choose, it's a sure thing that you'll be able to grill great fish!

The Fire

Charcoal fires can be started in any of several safe, ecologically sound ways. The charcoal is always mounded onto the lower fire grate of the grill except when using a charcoal chimney. When the fire is hot, spread the coals out in an even layer on the fire grate. This is the direct cooking area. The following items will aid you in easy fire starting:

The *charcoal chimney* is a straight upright cylindrical metal cannister. Fill the chimney with approximately 15-20 briquettes. Place it on a nonflammable surface, such as concrete or the top of the grill, and put crumpled paper in the bottom. Light the paper. After about 15 minutes, the coals will be hot. Empty the coals onto the lower fire rack of the grill.

The *electric starter* is the easiest way to start a fire. You'll probably need an outdoor electrical outlet or extension cord. Place the coil on the lower rack of the grill and stack charcoal on top of it. Plug it in and the fire will start in about 10 minutes. Remove the coil and let the starter cool on a nonflammable surface, out of the reach of children and pets.

Solid starters are compressed wood blocks or sticks treated with flammable substances, such as paraffin. They are easy to ignite and don't give off a chemical odor. Two or three will easily light the charcoal; set them on top of or beside the briquettes and ignite.

Gel fire starter is relatively new on the market. It's a non-petroleum fire starter that you squeeze onto your charcoal according to manufacturer's directions and then light.

Grilling Temperature

Fish is grilled directly over hot to medium-hot fires, depending on the distance your grill rack sits from the fire. The fire is ready when the flame has subsided and the coals are glowing red and just beginning to ash over. You can recognize medium-hot fire when the coals are no longer red, but ashen. Another test to gauge the temperature is to hold your hand 5 inches above the heat source. If you can only hold it there for about 2 seconds, your fire is hot; 3 to 4 seconds is a medium-hot fire, and 5 to 6 seconds is a low fire. Make sure that the grill rack is clean and lightly brushed with vegetable oil to prevent sticking.

Grilling Time

Estimating grilling times will be a challenge, because the time required to cook a fish varies due to the heat of the fire, the type of coals used, and the distance your heat source is from the grill. Use the suggested cooking times given in each recipe but also watch your fish while it's cooking—when the color turns opaque and the flesh just begins to flake when tested with a fork, it's done. The general rule of thumb is to cook 10 minutes per inch thick.

The Utensils

Several basic tools make grilling fish easier. A local restaurant supply store will be a good source for finding the items listed, and professional utensils are superior in quality and durability. Long handles are preferable on everything, to keep you a safe distance from the fire.

A stiff *wire brush* with a scraper makes cleaning the grill a simple job (tackle this while the grill is still warm).

Use a natural-bristled *basting brush* to put oil on the grill and to baste the fish during grilling.

Grill toppers are grates placed on top of the grill to accommodate small or delicate items, such as fish fillets, scallops, shrimp, and vegetables. Always grease the grill topper before using so fish won't stick.

Hinged *grill baskets* or *fish baskets* hold foods in place and make turning an easy process. Grease the baskets before using.

Grill woks, one of the newest additions to grilling gadgetry, make "stir-grilling" possible. The wok has holes to let in smoky flavor and it sits directly on top of the grill. Stir-grill marinated fish and vegetables by tossing with wooden paddles. The grill wok enables totally oil-free cooking and is sure to become a staple with health-conscious grill chefs.

Heat resistant mitts offer the best hand protection, especially when you need to touch any hot metals during the grilling process.

Long-handled, spring-loaded *tongs* are easier to use than the scissor type. They are great for turning shrimp, scallops, sliced vegetables, and skewers.

Keep a *spray bottle* or pan filled with water handy to douse flare-ups. A garden hose within quick reaching distance can substitute, but make sure the water is turned on!

Skewers—wood or metal—allow smaller items to be threaded loosely together and then placed on grill to cook. Wooden or bamboo skewers should be soaked for 20-30 minutes before using so the ends won't char during grilling. Flat metal skewers are preferred, so that cubed food doesn't spin while turning.

A long, wooden-handled offset *spatula* with a 5- to 6-inch blade is essential for turning fish fillets. Grease it well to avoid sticking.

Flavor Enhancements

Fish and seafood pick up marinade flavors quickly. Marinating for 15 minutes to an hour should be sufficient. Do not overmarinate, or fish flesh will break down and become mushy. At their simplest, marinades and bastes can be a light application of oil with salt and pepper seasoning. The recipes in this book have accompanying bastes or marinade, but also use the Marinades, Butters, Sauces, and Salsas section to experiment and find your favorite flavoring for fish on the grill.

Woods and herbs added to the grill fire offer another means of flavor enhancement. Fish cooks so quickly over a hot fire that your addition of soaked wood chips or herbs will not penetrate as effectively as will slow smoking with a closed lid grill. But, the heavenly odor in your backyard is worth giving it a try. So choose hardwoods that burn hot like mesquite or oak. Fruit woods are also nice; try cherry, apple, or grapevines. Wood chips are best for quick cooking. Soak them for about 30 minutes prior to grilling or keep a plastic container filled with wood chips in water. Then throw a handful on the fire. If you want more smoke flavor while you're grilling the fish, simply close the lid for a few minutes.

Dried herbs also can be thrown onto the fire. Try thick-stalked varieties such as fennel or basil. Again, this is more an aromatic experience for the grillers than it is for the fish, but it's fun and adds to the outdoor atmosphere, so if it pleases you, do it!

FISH SUBSTITUTION GUIDE FOR THE GRILL

Use this guide to help you select the freshest fish at the market. If your fish choice is not available, substitute another fish from the same category.

	Mild Flavor	Moderate Flavor	Full Flavor
Firm Texture	Lobster Monkfish Softshell crab Shrimp	John Dory Salmon (steaks) Shark Sturgeon	Marlin Ono Swordfish Tuna
Medium Firm Texture	Catfish (whole) Grouper Haddock Halibut Scallops Sea bass Snapper Striped bass Tilefish Wolf fish	Mahi-mahi Ocean perch/ rockfish Pompano Porgy Rainbow trout Salmon (fillets) Tilapia Walleye pike	Amberjack Bluefish Buffalo fish King fish Mackerel Sablefish Yellowtail
Delicate Texture	Catfish (fillets) Cod Orange roughy Sea trout	Mullet Whiting/hake	Butterfish

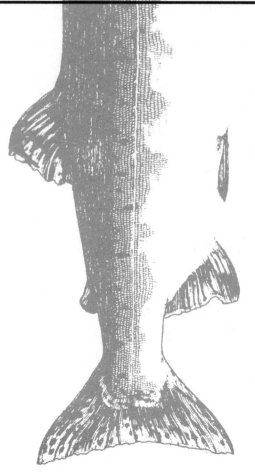

MARINADES, BUTTERS, SAUCES, AND SALSAS

Herb Mix for Fish

4 teaspoons dried lemon peel
3 teaspoons dried tarragon
3 teaspoons dried chervil
2-1/2 teaspoons garlic powder
2-1/2 teaspoons freshly ground pepper
3/4 teaspoons salt
1/2 teaspoon red pepper flakes

Combine all ingredients. Lightly oil fish before coating with mixture. Use about 1 teaspoon herb mix per serving. The longer the coating remains on fish, the more pungent the flavor will be. Keeps in a tightly covered glass jar for several weeks.

Makes about 1/3 cup

Blackened Seasoning

2 teaspoons lemon pepper marinade
1 teaspoon garlic powder
1 tablespoon paprika
1 teaspoon dried parsley flakes
1 teaspoon dried basil
1/2 teaspoon freshly ground pepper
1/2 teaspoon cayenne pepper
1/2 teaspoon salt

Combine all ingredients. Sprinkle 1/2 to 1 teaspoon of mix on a lightly oiled fillet of red snapper, catfish, tuna or fish of your choice. Keeps in a tightly covered glass jar for several weeks.

Makes about 1/4 cup

Mustard Butter

1/2 cup (1 stick) butter
1/4 cup lemon juice
2 tablespoons coarse-grain mustard
2 teaspoons Worcestershire sauce
1/2 teaspoon hot pepper sauce
2 cloves garlic, minced
Salt and freshly ground pepper to taste

In a small saucepan, melt butter. Whisk in remaining ingredients. Ready to use as a baste at this point or may be chilled and reheated later.

Makes about 1 cup

Herb Butter

1/2 cup (1 stick) butter, softened
1 teaspoon lemon juice
1 tablespoon finely minced fresh herbs or 3/4 teaspoon
 dried (any combination of chives, thyme, rosemary,
 basil, or tarragon)

Combine all ingredients. Shape butter into a roll. Wrap in waxed paper and chill. Slice a pat of butter and place on hot-off-the-grill fish.

Makes about 1/2 cup

Pistachio Butter

1/2 cup (1 stick) butter, softened
1/2 cup whole pistachio nuts, shells on
Salt to taste

Shell pistachios and parboil for 1 minute. Remove the skins and finely grind in food processor or by hand. Mix with softened butter and add salt to taste. Shape into a roll in waxed paper and chill. Serve a pat on monkfish, lobster, or fish of your choice.

Makes about 1/2 cup

Whipped Onion Butter

1/2 cup (1 stick) butter, softened
1 teaspoon Worcestershire sauce
1/4 teaspoon dry mustard
1/4 teaspoon cracked pepper
2 tablespoons minced onion
2 tablespoons snipped parsley

Combine butter, Worcestershire sauce, mustard, and pepper. Cream until fluffy. Add onion and parsley and chill. Serve a dollop on fish of your choice.

Makes about 3/4 cup

Caviar Mayonnaise

1/2 cup mayonnaise
2 tablespoons lemon juice
2 tablespoons salmon caviar

Combine mayonnaise and lemon juice, then gently stir in caviar. Chill. Serve a dollop on your favorite fish.

Makes about 3/4 cup

Herbed Mayonnaise

1 cup mayonnaise
4 tablespoons chopped fresh herbs (chives, parsley, tarragon, or dill)

Combine all ingredients and chill. Serve a dollop on your favorite fish.

Makes about 1 cup

Tartar Sauce

1/2 cup mayonnaise
2 tablespoons sweet pickle relish
1 tablespoon grated onion
1/2 teaspoon Worcestershire sauce
Salt and freshly ground pepper to taste

Combine all ingredients and blend well. Chill before serving with your favorite fish.

Makes about 3/4 cup

Horseradish Sauce

6 tablespoons mayonnaise
1 tablespoon horseradish
1/2 teaspoon dry mustard

Combine all ingredients and chill. Serve alongside your choice of shellfish.

Makes about 1/2 cup

Cucumber Sauce

1 cup minced cucumber
1 cup sour cream
Dill to taste
1/2 teaspoon salt

Drain cucumber for 1 to 2 hours. Add sour cream, dill, and salt. Chill. Serve with fish or as a salad dressing.

Makes 2 cups

Quick Corn Relish

1 (11-ounce) can Mexicorn
1/4 cup chopped onion
1/4 cup Italian dressing

Combine all ingredients and chill for a minimum of 2 hours or overnight.

Makes about 1-1/2 cups

Pico de Gallo

3 ripe avocados, peeled and chopped
2 ripe tomatoes, peeled and chopped
1 small onion, chopped
2 cloves garlic, minced
1 bunch cilantro, minced
1 jalapeño pepper, seeded and finely chopped
1/4 cup lime juice
Salt and freshly ground pepper to taste

Combine all ingredients and lightly toss. Chill before serving.

Makes 2–3 cups

Fresh Garden Relish

4 medium tomatoes, chopped
1 green bell pepper, chopped
1 yellow bell pepper, chopped
1/4 cup snipped chives
1/2 cup minced red onion
1 minced jalapeño pepper
1-1/2 teaspoons salt
1/2 teaspoon freshly ground pepper

Combine all ingredients. Cover and chill overnight.

Makes 5–6 cups

Roasted Red Pepper and Corn Salsa

1 large red bell pepper
2 tablespoons red wine vinegar
4 tablespoons olive oil
1/2 cup sour cream
1 clove garlic, minced
Salt and freshly ground pepper to taste
Pinch of cayenne pepper
3/4 cup cooked corn kernels
2 tablespoons fresh chopped basil
2 tablespoons fresh chopped cilantro

Halve and seed bell pepper. Char outside skin, either by broiling in oven or by placing skin-side down on grill over hot fire. Place charred peppers in a paper bag for 5 to 10 minutes, then peel off charred skin. Dice pepper and set aside.

Thoroughly combine vinegar and oil in a blender or food processor. Transfer to a bowl and stir in sour cream, garlic, salt, and peppers. Add corn, basil, and cilantro and chill. Flavors are best if served at room temperature.

Makes about 2 cups

FAST FRESH RECIPES
FOR FISH AND SEAFOOD

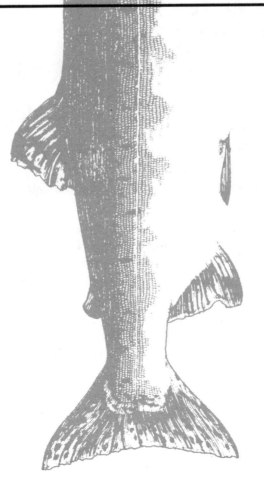

Mesquite Grilled Amberjack with Avocado-Corn Salsa

4 (6-8-ounce) amberjack fillets
1-2 tablespoons olive oil
Salt to taste
Freshly ground red, green, and black peppercorns to taste

Avocado-Corn Salsa:
2 large ripe avocados
1 cup fresh corn kernels or thawed frozen corn
1/4 cut chopped onion
2 cloves garlic, minced
1 tablespoon chopped cilantro
1/4 teaspoon red pepper flakes
Juice of 1 lime
Salt to taste

To prepare salsa, chop avocados into 1/2-inch cubes and transfer to a bowl. Add remaining ingredients and gently stir together. Let sit for 1 hour before serving.

Lightly brush fillets with oil and season to taste with peppers.

Soak a handful of mesquite wood chips. When ready to grill fish, throw wood chips onto hot coals. Grill for 5 minutes per side. Cover grill for a smokier flavor while fillets are cooking. Serve with avocado-corn salsa.

Serves 4

Barbecued Bass Fillets and Kath's Sweet 'n' Sour Broccoli

2 pounds freshwater bass fillets
1 small red onion, sliced
Juice of 2 lemons
Salt and freshly ground pepper to taste
Paprika to taste

Place fillets in a single layer in a disposable aluminum pan. Cover fillets with onion slices, then generously sprinkle lemon juice over fillets and onions. Season with salt, pepper, and paprika. Place pan on grill. Cook over hot coals for about 5 minutes per side or until fish flakes easily.

Serves 4

Kath's Sweet 'n' Sour Broccoli

1 bunch broccoli
1 cup sour cream
1-1/2 tablespoons chopped onion
1-1/2 teaspoons celery seed
1/4 teaspoon salt
1 teaspoon sugar
2 tablespoons vinegar
1 teaspoon horseradish

Cook broccoli until tender but crisp, then chill.

Blend remaining ingredients and refrigerate. When ready to serve, pour sour cream mixture over chilled broccoli.

Serves 4

Sea Bass with Pesto Sauce

4 (6-ounce) sea bass fillets
Juice of 1 lemon
Freshly ground pepper to taste
1–2 tablespoons olive oil
Sliced tomatoes

Pesto Sauce:
2 cups torn, fresh basil leaves
1/2 cup pine nuts
1 clove garlic, crushed
1/2 cup grated Parmesan cheese
3/4 cup olive oil

To prepare sauce, in a food processor puree basil leaves, pine nuts, garlic, and 1/4 cup Parmesan cheese. Gradually add oil and remaining cheese. Refrigerate, then bring to room temperature before serving.

Drizzle lemon juice over fillets and season with pepper. Let stand for 15 minutes. Lightly brush with olive oil and grill over hot coals for 4 to 5 minutes per side, until fish flakes. Serve with pesto and sliced tomatoes.

Serves 4

Marinated Striped Bass Steaks

4 (6–8-ounce) striped bass steaks

Marinade:
1/4 cup olive oil
4 tablespoons lemon juice
2 tablespoons sherry
2 tablespoons Pickapeppa sauce
1 clove garlic, minced
Salt and freshly ground pepper to taste

Place steaks in a shallow glass dish. Combine marinade ingredients and pour over fish. Refrigerate for 30 minutes to 1 hour.

Remove steaks from marinade and reserve liquid. Grill over hot coals for 5 to 6 minutes each side, basting frequently with reserved marinade. Serve with additional Pickapeppa sauce on the side.

Serves 4

Boston Bluefish with Spicy Sliced Tomatoes

6 Boston bluefish fillets (about 2 pounds)
6 large tomatoes, sliced to medium thickness
1 large green pepper, sliced into thin rings
1 large red onion, sliced into thin rings
1/2 cup chopped fresh parsley

Marinade:
1-1/2 cups cider vinegar
1/2 cup water
3 tablespoons sugar
3 teaspoons celery salt
2 teaspoons dry mustard
1/4 teaspoon freshly ground black pepper
1/4 teaspoon cayenne pepper

Combine all marinade ingredients in a saucepan. Boil for 1 minute. Cool.

Place fillets in a shallow glass dish. Pour 1 cup of marinade over fish and refrigerate for 1 hour. Reserve remaining cup of marinade for tomatoes.

Grill fillets over hot coals for 4 to 5 minutes per side.

On each dinner plate, alternate tomato slices with green pepper and onion rings. Place a fillet on each plate and spoon marinade over all. Garnish with parsley and serve.

Serves 6

Salsa Catfish and Southern-Fried Hush Puppies

6 farm-raised catfish fillets or steaks
Scant 1/2 teaspoon white pepper
3/4 teaspoon garlic salt
2 cups favorite salsa

Sprinkle fillets with pepper and garlic salt. Place in a well-greased fish grilling basket over hot coals. Grill for 10 minutes per inch of thickness, turning once, until fish flakes easily. Serve with salsa and **Southern-Fried Hush Puppies**.

Serves 6

This recipe appears courtesy of the Catfish Institute.

Southern-Fried Hush Puppies

2 cups cornmeal
1 tablespoon flour
1 teaspoon salt
1 teaspoon baking powder
1/2 teaspoon baking soda
4 tablespoons finely chopped onion
1 cup buttermilk
1 large egg
2 cups oil

In a large bowl, combine dry ingredients. Add onion and buttermilk. Beat egg and add last. In a large, deep skillet, heat oil. When hot, drop batter by spoonfuls into oil. Turn and cook until golden brown. Serve immediately.

Serves 6

Stir-Grilled Catfish

4 farm-raised catfish fillets
12 cherry tomatoes
1 red onion, halved then quartered
1 green pepper, sliced
1 zucchini, sliced
1 cup sliced mushrooms

Vinaigrette Marinade:
1/2 cup olive oil
2 tablespoons minced shallots
2 teaspoons Dijon mustard
1 tablespoon lemon juice
3 tablespoons red wine vinegar
Salt and freshly ground pepper to taste

To prepare marinade, in a wooden bowl or food processor, mix shallots, mustard, lemon juice, vinegar, salt, and pepper. Add oil in a slow steady stream until well incorporated. Set aside.

Slice catfish fillets into 1/2-inch strips and place with vegetables in a large bowl. Pour vinaigrette marinade over all and marinate for 1 hour in refrigerator. Transfer ingredients to a grill wok and drain briefly over sink. Stir-grill in wok over hot coals for 8 to 10 minutes, and then serve.

Serves 4

Stir-grill recipes are easily varied by substituting different fish and vegetables. Eye appeal is key, so let color as well as taste be your guide.

Grilled Whole Catfish and Aunt Laretta's Slaw

4 (2/3-pound) dressed catfish
1 lemon, sliced
1 medium onion, sliced
1/2 cup vegetable oil
1/4 cup lemon juice
Salt and freshly ground pepper to taste

Place slices of lemon and onion in the cavity of each fish. Combine oil, lemon juice, salt, and pepper in a small bowl for basting. Place fish in a well-greased grilling basket or grill topper. Grill fish over medium-hot coals for 12 minutes per side or until fish flakes easily, basting often. Serve with **Aunt Laretta's Slaw**.

Serves 6

Aunt Laretta's Slaw

1 medium cabbage, shredded
1/2 onion, grated
1-1/2 teaspoons salt
1 teaspoon celery seed
1/2 teaspoon freshly ground pepper
8 slices bacon, fried and crumbled
1 cup Italian dressing

Combine all ingredients except bacon and dressing and refrigerate. When ready to serve, add bacon and toss with Italian dressing.

Serves 6–8

Softshell Crabs with Tangy Seafood Sauce

8 softshell crabs (in season from mid-May through mid-August)
4 tablespoons butter
4 tablespoons lemon juice

Tangy Seafood Sauce:
1/2 cup mayonnaise
1/3 cup chili sauce
1-1/2 tablespoons horseradish
1/2 teaspoon dry mustard

Melt butter and stir in lemon juice. Reserve for basting.

To prepare sauce, combine mayonnaise, chili sauce, horseradish, and mustard. Refrigerate until ready to serve.

Grill softshell crabs over hot coals for 7 to 8 minutes per side, basting several times while grilling. Serve warm with sauce.

Serves 4

Onion-Buttered Cod Fillets

4 (6-ounce) cod fillets
1–2 tablespoons olive oil
1 teaspoon salt
1/2 teaspoon freshly ground pepper
1 lemon, cut into wedges

Baste:
3 tablespoons butter or margarine
1 medium onion, finely chopped
1/4 cup dry white wine

Brush fish with olive oil and season with salt and pepper.

To prepare baste, in a medium-sized skillet sauté onions in butter. Add white wine. Simmer briefly, then remove from heat and reserve.

Arrange fillets on a greased grill topper and place on grill over hot coals. Grill for approximately 4 to 5 minutes per side, brushing with marinade while grilling. Serve with lemon wedges.

Serves 4

Parslied new potatoes would blend well as a side dish with this onion-flavored baste.

Cod with Caper-Parsley Sauce

4 (6-ounce) cod fillets
1–2 tablespoons oil
Salt and freshly ground pepper to taste

Caper-Parsley Sauce:
3 tablespoons white vinegar
1 cup chopped parsley
2 cloves garlic, minced
4 tablespoons tiny capers
1 tablespoon chopped onion
1 tablespoon Dijon mustard
2/3 cup olive oil

To make sauce, in a food processor or blender puree vinegar, parsley, garlic, capers, onion, and mustard. Add oil a drop at a time while machine is running to make a thick green sauce. Chill.

Brush fish lightly with oil and sprinkle with salt and pepper. Grill over hot coals for 4 to 5 minutes per side. Spoon several tablespoons of sauce onto each fillet and serve.

Serves 4

Tandoori Stir-Grilled Fish

3 pounds cod or haddock chunks

Yogurt Marinade:
1 cup yogurt
4 or 5 cloves garlic, minced
1 (2-inch) piece fresh ginger
1 teaspoon cayenne pepper
2 teaspoons ground cumin
2 teaspoons ground coriander
1 teaspoon salt
4 tablespoons vegetable oil

For yogurt marinade, peel ginger and grate or process to a paste. Combine remaining ingredients and blend well. Add fish chunks and marinate for 30 minutes.

Pour mixture ingredients into a greased grill wok. Place over sink and partially drain. Grill over hot coals for 6 to 8 minutes or until fish flakes easily.

Serves 8

This recipe appears courtesy of Judith Fertig, author of Kansas City Gold. Judith says, "This yogurt and Indian spice marinade keeps fish moist and flavorful. It's also a versatile dish to use on tuna steaks, skewered shrimp or scallops, and even chicken breasts."

Herb-Grilled Grouper

4 (6-ounce) grouper fillets
1 lemon, cut into wedges

Marinade:
1/3 cup olive oil
1/4 cup minced herbs (any combination of parsley, thyme, marjoram, and Greek oregano)
3-1/2 tablespoons fresh lemon juice
3 large cloves garlic, crushed
1 tablespoon minced shallot or green onion
Salt and freshly ground pepper to taste

Combine marinade ingredients and pour over fillets in a glass dish. Marinate for several hours in the refrigerator, stirring occasionally.

Place fillets on a greased grill topper and grill over hot coals for 3 to 4 minutes per side, basting with remaining marinade while cooking. Serve with lemon wedges on the side.

Serves 4

Grouper with Dilled Cucumber Sauce

2 (6-ounce) grouper fillets
3 tablespoons butter
1 tablespoon lemon juice
2 sprigs fresh dill

Dilled Cucumber Sauce:
1 cup peeled, seeded and diced cucumber
1/4 cup sliced green onions
1/4 cup oil
1 tablespoon lemon juice
2 sprigs fresh dill or 1 teaspoon dried
1/2 teaspoon salt
Freshly ground pepper to taste

In a blender or food processor, combine all sauce ingredients and puree. Refrigerate.

Melt butter in a small saucepan and add lemon juice. Set aside.

Grill fillets over hot coals for 5 minutes per side. Baste while cooking, using sprigs of dill to brush on lemon butter. Serve with cucumber sauce.

Serves 2

The Dilled Cucumber Sauce is also an excellent accompaniment to grilled or steamed vegetables.

Haddock with Hazelnut Lime Butter

4 (6–8-ounce) haddock fillets
4 tablespoons oil
Salt and freshly ground pepper to taste

Hazelnut Lime Butter:
1/4 cup hazelnuts
Zest of 1 lime
Juice of 1/2 lime
1/4 cup (1/2 stick) unsalted butter, softened

To make butter, spread hazelnuts on a baking sheet and toast in a 350-degree oven for about 5 minutes. (Watch carefully to avoid burning.) Finely grind nuts in a food processor and combine with lime zest, lime juice, and butter. (*Note:* This keeps in the refrigerator for 3 to 4 days. Bring to room temperature before serving.)

Coat salmon with oil and season with salt and pepper. Grill over hot coals for approximately 3 to 5 minutes per side. Serve with a dollop of hazelnut lime butter.

Serves 4

This recipe appears courtesy of Brenda Burns, chef-owner of Californos restaurant in Kansas City, Missouri.

Rosemary Dijon Halibut and Lemon Rice

4 (6–8-ounce) halibut fillets

Marinade:
3/4 cup olive oil
2 tablespoons Dijon mustard
2 teaspoons horseradish
Juice of 1 lemon
1 teaspoon fresh rosemary or 3/4 teaspoon dried
Salt and freshly ground pepper to taste

Combine marinade ingredients and marinate fish in mixture for at least 2 hours. Drain marinade and reserve for basting. Place fillets on a greased grill topper and grill over hot coals for 4 to 5 minutes per side, basting often with reserved marinade. Serve with **Lemon Rice**.

Serves 4

Lemon Rice

2 tablespoons butter
Zest and juice of 1 lemon
1 cup uncooked white rice
2 cups water
1/2 cup white wine
1 teaspoon salt

Melt butter in a medium pot, then add lemon zest and rice. Sauté for 5 minutes until rice is opaque. Add water, wine, and salt. Bring to a boil, cover, then simmer 40 minutes or until liquid is absorbed. Add lemon juice and fluff with a fork.

Serves 4

Halibut Fillet with Red Pepper Beurre Blanc

4–6 (7–8-ounce) halibut fillets
1–3 tablespoons olive oil

Beurre Blanc:
1/2 cup white wine
1 tablespoon tarragon vinegar
1 shallot, diced
1 medium red bell pepper, chopped
1/4 cup heavy cream
1 cup (2 sticks) unsalted butter, chilled
Salt to taste

To prepare beurre blanc, first combine wine, vinegar, shallot, and red pepper. Bring to a slow boil and reduce until 2 tablespoons of liquid remain. Add cream and boil for 2 minutes. Lower heat and whisk in butter a little at a time until all butter is incorporated. Remove from heat and place sauce in a blender on medium speed for 1 minute. Strain, then season with salt. Set aside.

Brush fillets with olive oil and grill over hot coals for 4 to 5 minutes per each side. Serve with beurre blanc spooned over fillets.

Serves 4

This recipe appears courtesy of Joe D's Wine Bar & Cafe in Kansas City, Missouri.

Stir-Grilled Seafood Tacos

1-1/2 pounds halibut chunks
2–3 tablespoons Cajun spice
2 cups shredded cabbage
1 cup shredded red cabbage
1/4 cup herb vinegar
1/4 cup sour cream
6 green onions, finely chopped
1/2 teaspoon salt
2 lemons, halved
8 flour tortillas
1-1/2 cups salsa
1-1/2 cups tartar sauce
1-1/2 cups guacamole

Season halibut chunks with Cajun spice. Stir-grill over hot coals in a well-greased grill wok for 8 to 10 minutes, tossing while cooking.

Combine cabbages in a large bowl. In a small bowl, combine vinegar, sour cream, green onions, and salt. Blend and toss with cabbage.

For each tortilla, fill with 1/3 cup of cabbage mixture and 4 or 5 pieces of halibut. Serve with lemons, salsa, tartar sauce, and guacamole on the side.

Serves 4

Perfect with a margarita and taco chips!

Grilled John Dory with Veggies

4 (6-ounce) John Dory fillets
2 tablespoons butter, softened
1 cup chopped fresh tomato
1 cup chopped onion
1/2 cup chopped fresh parsley
1/2 cup Italian dressing

Spice Rub:
2 tablespoons paprika
1 tablespoon garlic powder
1 tablespoon salt
1 tablespoon freshly ground pepper
1/2 tablespoon crushed dried tarragon
1/4 teaspoon cayenne pepper

To prepare vegetables, grease a sheet of foil with butter and top with tomato, onion, and parsley. Fold and seal foil into a packet and poke several holes in the top. Set aside.

Combine spice rub ingredients and set aside.

Marinate fillets in Italian dressing for 1 hour, refrigerated. Remove from marinade and sprinkle both sides with spice rub. Place fillets and foil packet of vegetables on a grill topper and grill over medium hot coals for 8 to 10 minutes (4 to 5 minutes per side for fillets). Serve fish with chopped grilled vegetables on the side.

Serves 4

This recipe appears courtesy of Donnie Morris, an award-winning grill master from Memphis, Tennessee, who also recommends using catfish for this recipe.

Pernod-Buttered Lobster Tails

4 (8-ounce) rock lobster tails
4 tablespoons butter, melted

Pernod Butter:
1/2 cup (1 stick) butter
2 tablespoons Pernod liqueur
2 tablespoons crushed tarragon

Make Pernod butter by combining all ingredients. Set aside.

Cut top membrane from lobster tails and discard. Loosen meat from shell and brush with melted butter.

Put tails on grill, cut-side down, and cook for 2 to 3 minutes. Turn tails and grill until done, 7 to 9 minutes. The shell may char. Serve with Pernod butter.

Serves 4

This recipe appears courtesy of Donnie Morris, who says, "This is so good you'll want to slap your grandmaw!"

Mahi Mahi with Kiwi Sauce

6 (6–8-ounce) mahi mahi fillets
1–2 tablespoons oil
Salt and freshly ground pepper to taste
1 kiwi, peeled and sliced, for garnish

Kiwi Sauce:
3 kiwis, peeled
1 teaspoon curry powder
1 teaspoon salt

To make sauce, puree kiwis with curry powder and salt. Chill before serving.

Brush fillets with oil and season to taste. Arrange on a grill topper and grill over hot coals for approximately 5 minutes per side. Garnish with kiwi slices and serve with sauce.

Serves 6

Almond-Buttered Mahi Mahi

8 (4-ounce) mahi mahi fillets
3/4 cup vegetable oil
Salt and freshly ground pepper to taste

Almond Butter:
1/2 cup (1 stick) butter
4 ounces almonds, sliced

Coat fish with oil and season with salt and pepper. Set aside.

To make almond butter, melt butter in a small skillet, add almonds, and brown. Set aside.

Grill fillets on a greased grill topper over hot coals for 5 minutes per side. Serve 2 fillets per person and top with almond butter.

Serves 4

Almond butter is versatile. Try substituting trout, walleye, or whitefish for the mahi mahi.

Teriyaki Stir-Grilled Mahi Mahi with Island Salsa

1-1/2 pounds mahi mahi, cubed
3/4 cup teriyaki sauce
1 tablespoon dry sherry
1 clove garlic, minced

Island Salsa:
1 each papaya, mango, grapefruit, and orange, peeled and
   diced
1/2 red onion, diced
1/2 green pepper, diced
1/2 jalapeño pepper, seeded and minced
1/4 cup finely chopped cilantro
1/4 cup finely chopped fresh mint leaves
1 tablespoon lime juice
1 tablespoon lemon juice
1/2 to 1 teaspoon red pepper flakes

To prepare salsa, combine all ingredients and refrigerate for 1 hour. Serve at room temperature.

Place cubed fish in plastic bag or nonmetallic container and add teriyaki sauce, sherry, and garlic. Marinate at least 30 minutes.

Pour fish into grill wok and drain over sink. Place wok on top of grill over hot coals and stir-grill 7 to 8 minutes, tossing with wooden paddles. Close lid for an additional 2 to 3 minutes to heat thoroughly. Serve with salsa on the side.

Serves 4

Grilled Mackerel with Anchovy and Rosemary

2 (1-pound) mackerels, dressed
4 tablespoons butter, melted
4 anchovy fillets
1/2 teaspoon dried rosemary
Parsley sprigs for garnish
Lemon wedges for garnish

Split each mackerel down the back and fold open. Brush both sides with melted butter. Place skin-side down on an oiled grill topper. Arrange 2 anchovy fillets on flesh of each mackerel and sprinkle with 1/4 teaspoon rosemary.

Place grill topper over hot coals and cook fish for 10 minutes or until flesh flakes easily. Do not turn. (Mackerel are so thin you don't have to turn them.) Serve garnished with parsley and lemon wedges.

Serves 2

Marlin Steaks with Balsamic Vinegar and Grilled Garden Onions

2 (14–16-ounce) marlin steaks
Salt and lemon pepper to taste
3 tablespoons unsalted butter
1/3 cup balsamic vinegar

Season steaks with salt and lemon pepper. Let stand for 10 to 15 minutes.

Melt butter and whisk in balsamic vinegar. Grill steaks over hot coals for 5 minutes per side, basting with butter mixture. Serve with **Grilled Garden Onions**.

Serves 4

Balsamic vinegar gives this fish a sweet and sour flavor.

Grilled Garden Onions

4-6 onions, preferably fresh from the garden

Leave outer skin intact and place onions on top of hot grill for 10 to 15 minutes. Outer skin will char, inside flesh will be soft. Remove charred outer skin and serve.

Serves 4

Monkfish with Jalapeño Peppers and Cilantro

1-1/2 pounds monkfish fillet
1 medium zucchini, sliced into 1/8-inch circles
8 mushrooms, cleaned
1 red onion, skinned, quartered and separated

Marinade:
1 cup chili sauce
1 tablespoon cider vinegar
3 green onions, minced (tops included)
1-1/2 teaspoons minced fresh jalapeño peppers, seeded
1/4 teaspoon chili powder
1/4 teaspoon freshly ground pepper
1-1/2 teaspoons liquid smoke
3 tablespoons minced fresh cilantro

To prepare marinade, combine all ingredients and refrigerate for 4 hours. Cut monkfish into 1-inch cubes and marinate in chili-vinegar mixture for 4 hours in refrigerator or overnight, stirring occasionally. Add the vegetables 2 hours before skewering.

Alternate fish and vegetables on skewers, allowing 2 skewers per person. Grill kabobs over medium heat for 8 to 10 minutes, turning every 2 minutes. Do not overcook or fish will get tough. Let stand, loosely covered in a warm place, for 5 minutes before serving.

Serves 4

This recipe appears courtesy of Leslie Bloom, author of Barbeque: Sizzling Fireside Know-How.

Lemon-Lime Monkfish

1 pound monkfish, skinned and trimmed
1 lemon, sliced
1 lime, sliced

Marinade:
Juice of 1 lemon
Juice of 1 lime
2/3 cup olive oil
3 cloves garlic, minced
1 bunch fresh basil leaves, chopped
Salt and freshly ground pepper to taste

To prepare marinade, combine lemon and lime juice with olive oil, stirring constantly until thoroughly blended. Add garlic, basil, salt, and pepper. Set aside.

Cut fish into bite-sized cubes and place in a shallow glass dish with sliced lemon and lime slices. Pour marinade over all and marinate in refrigerator for 1 hour.

Place fish plus lemon and lime slices in a grill wok, letting marinade drain over sink. Put wok on grill over hot coals. Toss fish and lemon-lime slices with wooden spoons for 3 to 5 minutes. Close grill lid and cook for 2 to 3 minutes more, then serve.

Serves 4

Citrus-Grilled Orange Roughy

4 (6–8-ounce) orange roughy fillets

Marinade:
1/2 cup olive oil
1/4 cup dry white wine
1 clove garlic, finely chopped
1/2 teaspoon red pepper flakes
1/2 teaspoon chopped parsley
1/4 teaspoon salt
1/4 teaspoon freshly ground pepper
Grated zest of 1 orange
Juice of 1 orange

Combine marinade ingredients and pour over fish in a glass dish. Cover and refrigerate for 1 hour.

Remove fish from marinade and reserve liquid for basting. Arrange fish, skin-side down, on a grill topper. Grill until fillets flake easily (about 5 minutes per side), basting with remaining marinade while cooking. Serve immediately.

Serves 4

Orange roughy fillets are a perfect example of fillets that are tapered and thin at one end. To avoid overcooking the tapered end, simply fold the tip over to create thickness.

Orange Roughy with Cantaloupe Salsa

4 (6–8-ounce) orange roughy fillets
2 tablespoons olive oil
Salt and freshly ground pepper to taste

Cantaloupe Salsa:
2 cups cantaloupe balls
Juice of 1/2 lime
1–2 tablespoons chopped mint leaves
1/4 teaspoon red pepper flakes
1 cup blueberries (optional)

Oil fillets and season with salt and pepper. Set aside.

Combine salsa ingredients. Gently toss and refrigerate.

Grill fillets over hot coals for approximately 4 to 5 minutes per side. Serve with salsa on the side.

Serves 4

Salsas are a great summer accompaniment because they're very flavorful and low in calories. Be creative with this one—substitute other melons for variety, or substitute cilantro for the mint leaves (a totally different taste).

Arkansas Trav'lers
Barbecued Oysters

36 raw oysters
Rock salt
Barbecue sauce

Topping:
1/2 cup (1 stick) butter, melted
1/2 teaspoon garlic powder
1/4 cup fine bread crumbs
1 teaspoon dried oregano
2 dashes hot pepper sauce
1 teaspoon chopped parsley
2 tablespoons minced onions

Arrange oysters on the half shell on a bed of rock salt in a disposable shallow aluminum pan. Combine topping ingredients and place 1 teaspoon of mixture on each oyster.

Place pan on the grill and cook over indirect heat with lots of hickory smoke (add soaked hickory chips to the coals) for approximately 30 minutes. Oysters are done when edges begin to curl. Serve as an appetizer with your favorite hot barbecue sauce.

Serves 6

This recipe appears courtesy of barbecue champion Jim Quessenberry.

Ocean Perch and Parmesan-Crusted Tomatoes

6 (6–8-ounce) ocean perch or rockfish fillets

Baste:
1/2 cup (1 stick) butter
1/2 teaspoon dried marjoram leaves
2 teaspoons lemon juice

To prepare baste, melt butter in a small saucepan and blend in marjoram and lemon juice. Set aside. Place fillets on a greased grill topper and grill over medium-hot coals for 4 to 5 minutes per side, basting frequently. Serve with **Parmesan-Crusted Tomatoes**.

Serves 6

Parmesan-Crusted Tomatoes

3 fresh tomatoes, halved
3 tablespoons sherry
3/4 teaspoon dill
3/4 teaspoon freshly ground pepper
1/4 cup mayonnaise
1/4 cup Parmesan cheese

Pierce tomato halves several times with a fork. Spoon 1/2 teaspoon sherry, 1/8 teaspoon dill, and 1/8 teaspoon pepper on each tomato half. Broil 2 to 3 minutes. Combine mayonnaise and Parmesan cheese, and spoon onto each tomato half. Broil 2 to 3 minutes more to lightly brown. Serve hot.

Serves 6

Grilled Pompano with Lime and Olive Oil

4 (8-ounce) pompano fillets
3 tablespoons vegetable oil
Salt and freshly cracked pepper to taste
1/4 cup extra-virgin olive oil
2 limes, halved
2 tablespoons chopped parsley

Rub fillets with oil and season with salt and pepper.

Place fillets skin-side up on a grill topper and grill over a medium-hot fire for 3 to 4 minutes. Turn over and cook for 2 to 3 minutes more, until fish is opaque all the way through.

Remove fillets from the grill, drizzle with olive oil, squeeze 1/2 lime over each, and sprinkle with chopped parsley.

Serves 4

This recipe appears courtesy of Chris Schlesinger, Ph.B., coauthor of The Thrill of the Grill.

Captain's Barbecued Salmon Fillets

8 (8-ounce) salmon fillets
1/2 cup salad oil
1 cup hot barbecue sauce
8 kiwis, peeled and sliced
8 sprigs fresh dill

Marinade:
1 cup soy sauce
2 teaspoons liquid smoke
1 tablespoon sugar
1 cup dry white wine
1 teaspoon minced fresh ginger
1 teaspoon freshly ground pepper
1 tablespoon sesame oil
1 teaspoon minced garlic

Combine marinade ingredients and stir well. Pour over fillets and marinate for 20 minutes.

Dredge marinated fillets in salad oil and place on a greased grill topper. Grill over hot coals 4 minutes and turn. Grill for 4 minutes, brush both sides with barbecue sauce, and then cook for an additional 1 to 2 minutes to set and heat sauce.

Place each fillet on a plate, garnished with fanned kiwi slices and dill sprigs.

Serves 8

This recipe appears courtesy of Captain Bilbo's restaurant in Memphis, Tennessee.

Pacific Rim Salmon Steaks

2 (12–14-ounce) salmon steaks, 1-inch thick

Marinade:
1/2 cup soy sauce
1/2 cup rice wine vinegar
2–3 cloves garlic, minced
2 tablespoons honey
1 teaspoon ground ginger
2 teaspoons toasted sesame seeds
1/2 teaspoon lemon pepper

Combine marinade ingredients and pour over salmon in a shallow glass dish. Marinate for 1 hour in refrigerator.

Grill steaks over hot coals for 5 minutes per side or until milky juice appears. Serve immediately.

Serves 4

Fresh steamed asparagus makes the perfect dinner partner for this fragrant fish.

Grilled Salmon Steaks with Mustard Dill Sauce

2 (12–14-ounce) salmon steaks
1–2 tablespoons olive oil
Lemon pepper to taste

Mustard Dill Sauce:
1/4 cup Dijon mustard
2 tablespoons sugar
1/4 cup white wine vinegar
4 sprigs fresh dill
1/2 cup olive oil

In a blender or food processor, combine all sauce ingredients except oil. Then add oil slowly to incorporate. Chill before serving.

Lightly brush steaks with olive oil and season with lemon pepper. Grill over hot coals for 5 to 6 minutes per side or until fish begins to flake. Serve with sauce.

Serves 4

Grilled Herbed Salmon

1-1/2 pounds boneless salmon fillets, skin intact

Marinade:
1/4 cup olive oil
1 tablespoon chopped thyme
1 tablespoon chopped marjoram
1/4 teaspoon red pepper flakes
1/4 cup dry white wine
1 tablespoon fresh lemon juice
2 tablespoons chopped parsley
Salt and freshly ground pepper to taste

Combine marinade ingredients and pour over salmon in a shallow glass dish. Marinate in refrigerator for 30 minutes.

Remove salmon for grilling. Pour marinade into a saucepan and bring to a boil. Boil for 1 minute, then remove from heat and set aside.

Place salmon on a grill topper, flesh-side down. Grill over hot coals for about 4 minutes, then turn over and continue grilling for 4 minutes more. Spoon cooked marinade over fillets and serve.

Serves 4

Stir-Grilled Salmon with Sugar Snap Peas

1 pound salmon steak or fillets
1/2 pound sugar snap peas
12 cherry tomatoes
1/2 red onion, sliced
3 cups cooked white rice

Marinade:
1/4 cup soy sauce
1/4 cup rice wine vinegar
2 tablespoons honey
4 cloves garlic, minced
1 teaspoon ginger
1 teaspoon sesame paste
3 cups cooked rice

Combine marinade ingredients in a glass bowl. Cube salmon and stem peas. Combine tomatoes and onion slices and marinate for 30 minutes or more.

Pour salmon mixture into a well-greased grill wok over the sink and partially drain liquid. Place wok over hot coals and stir-grill fish and vegetables with large wooden spoons for 6 to 8 minutes. Move wok to indirect-heat side of grill. Close lid on grill and cook for another 4 to 5 minutes. Serve with rice.

Serves 4

This is our favorite grill wok recipe. It combines texture, color, and taste at its best!

Barbequed Salmon Wrapped in Foil

4 (8-ounce) salmon fillets
1 carrot, finely chopped
1 stalk celery, finely chopped
5 mushrooms, finely chopped
1/2 teaspoon rosemary
4 tablespoons dry white wine

Grease four pieces of foil and place 1 fillet skin-side down, on each. Distribute chopped vegetables evenly over fillets, splash each with 1 tablespoon wine, and sprinkle 1/8 teaspoon rosemary across the tops. Tightly wrap each fillet in foil.

Grill foil packets for approximately 15 minutes over medium-hot coals. Place a packet on each of 4 dinner plates and serve.

Serves 4

This recipe appears courtesy of Jack Dugan, owner of The Gentleman's Choice restaurant in San Marcos, California.

Stir-Grilled Scallops

1 pound scallops
1/2 pound fresh mushroom caps
1 red bell pepper, julienned
2 cups cooked white rice

Marinade:
1/4 cup lemon juice
1/4 cup dry vermouth
1 clove garlic, finely minced
1/2 teaspoon salt
1/4 teaspoon freshly ground pepper
1/4 cup vegetable oil
2 tablespoons chopped fresh parsley

Combine marinade ingredients in a glass bowl. Add scallops, mushrooms, and red pepper, and marinate for 1 hour in refrigerator.

Pour scallops and mushrooms into a grill wok and drain over sink.

Place wok on the grill over hot coals and stir-grill for 7 to 8 minutes. Close lid tightly for 2 to 4 minutes to heat thoroughly. Serve over rice.

Serves 2

Seafood Skewers

1/2 pound scallops
1/2 pound green king prawns, shelled and deveined
Grated zest of 1 lemon
Juice of 1 lemon
Juice of 1/2 orange
3 tablespoons orange liqueur

Combine all ingredients in a bowl and marinate for 1 to 2 hours in the refrigerator. Remove seafood and reserve liquid for basting.

Thread scallops and prawns alternately onto 4 skewers. Grill, basting frequently with reserved marinade until just cooked, approximately 6 to 8 minutes.

Serves 2

For a colorful presentation, serve the skewers on a bed of thinly sliced oranges and cucumber.

Mako Shark with Cilantro-Lime Butter

6 (8-ounce) mako shark steaks
2 whole tomatoes, chopped
1 bunch green onions, chopped

Cilantro-Lime Butter:
1/2 bunch cilantro
Juice from 1–2 limes
1 pound (4 sticks) butter, softened

To prepare butter, rinse cilantro, chop coarsely, and place in a blender with lime juice. Puree, transfer to a mixing bowl, and combine with softened butter. Roll mixture into logs 1 inch in diameter. Wrap in waxed paper and chill or freeze.

Fold six 12- by 6-inch sheets of foil in half lengthwise. Cut into heart shapes. Place a steak on the right half of each heart. Top with a 1/4-inch thick slice of chilled cilantro-lime butter. Add 1/6 portion of chopped tomatoes and onions to other side of heart. Fold vegetable half over and roll edges of foil starting from left side and using small turns until envelope is firmly closed. Turn in point at end of fold to secure bag. Poke holes in top of foil packet and transfer to the grill. Cook over hot coals for 12 to 15 minutes. Using scissors, open and place heart shaped packets on plates and serve.

Serves 6

This recipe appears courtesy of Quail's Dinnerhouse in San Marcos, California. Permission arranged by Gwenn Jensen, author of San Diego Cuisine, *who says, "If shark is on the menu, I always order it because I feel it's my duty to keep my surfer friends safe!"*

Balsamic Grilled Shark

4 shark steaks

Marinade:
1/2 cup vegetable oil
1/4 cup balsamic vinegar
1-1/2 tablespoons sugar
1 tablespoon Worcestershire sauce
2 medium green onions, minced (tops included)
1 teaspoon dry mustard
1 medium clove garlic, minced
Hot pepper sauce to taste
Salt and freshly ground pepper to taste

Combine marinade ingredients and shark steaks in a plastic resealable bag or glass dish. Refrigerate for approximately 1 hour.

Bring shark to room temperature and remove from marinade. Reserve liquid. Grill steaks over hot coals for 4 minutes per side or until tender and browned, basting occasionally with marinade. Serve warm.

Serves 4

Contrary to the rule of grilling fish 10 minutes per inch of thickness, shark needs only 7 to 8 minutes per inch of thickness. Overcooking makes shark tough.

Lemon-Basil Basted Shrimp

24 jumbo shrimp (about 1-1/4 pounds), shelled and deveined

Marinade:
2 teaspoons finely chopped garlic
2 teaspoons finely chopped shallots
1-1/2 teaspoons Dijon mustard
1/3 cup dry white wine
1/3 cup fresh lemon juice
1/4 teaspoon freshly ground black pepper
1/2 cup olive oil
1/3 cup finely chopped fresh basil

Combine marinade ingredients. Add shrimp and toss until thoroughly coated. Marinate for 20 to 30 minutes.

Remove shrimp from marinade and pour remaining liquid into a saucepan. Arrange shrimp on a grill topper, keeping them flat. Cook for about 3 minutes or until shrimp can be lifted from grill without sticking. Turn over and cook for 2 minutes more.

Bring reserved marinade to a boil and simmer for 2 minutes. Arrange shrimp on a platter and spoon marinade over all. Serve immediately.

Serves 4

Perfect Barbecued Prawns

2 pounds prawns, shelled and deveined
Salt and freshly ground pepper to taste
Barbecue sauce

Marinade:
1 cup (2 sticks) unsalted butter
4 green onions, finely minced (tops included)
2 cloves garlic, finely minced
1 tablespoon finely chopped fresh parsley
1 cup dry white wine
2 tablespoons lemon juice

Melt butter in a saucepan over low heat. Sauté onions, garlic and parsley. Remove mixture from heat and add wine and lemon juice. Pour over prawns in a glass dish and marinate for 2 to 3 hours in refrigerator.

Remove prawns from marinade and season with salt and pepper. Place prawns on a greased grill topper over hot coals and cook for 2 to 3 minutes per side, basting with barbecue sauce. Serve immediately.

Serves 4–5

Shrimp on a Stick with Sherried Mustard Sauce

1–1-1/2 pounds shrimp, shelled and deveined
1/2 cup (1 stick) butter, melted
Juice of 2 lemons, quartered

Sherried Mustard Sauce:
1 cup mayonnaise
1/4 cup Dijon mustard
1 tablespoon dry sherry

Whisk sauce ingredients together and refrigerate until ready to serve.

Melt butter with lemon juice and set aside.

Thread shrimp onto wooden skewers that have been soaked in water. Grill over hot coals for 5 to 7 minutes, turning often and basting with lemon butter. Serve with sauce either drizzled over skewers or to the side.

Serves 4

Stir-Grilled Prawn Satay

3 pounds green king prawns, shelled and deveined

Satay Sauce:
2 cups coconut milk
1 small knob fresh ginger, chopped, or 1 teaspoon ground ginger
3 cloves garlic, crushed
Salt and freshly ground pepper to taste
1/4 cup soy sauce
3 teaspoons brown sugar
3 teaspoons chili powder
3 tablespoons lime juice

Combine all sauce ingredients. Place prawns in a glass dish, cover with sauce, and allow to marinate for at least 30 minutes.

Place prawns in a grill wok and drain over sink. Stir-grill over hot coals for 6 to 8 minutes or until prawns become opaque. Serve immediately.

Serves 6–8

Grilled Shrimp Scampi
with Garlic Sauce

2 pounds tiger shrimp, peeled and deveined

Garlic Sauce:
6 cloves garlic, minced
6 tablespoons olive oil
Juice of 2 oranges
2 tablespoons chopped parsley
Salt and freshly ground white pepper to taste

Combine sauce ingredients, pour over shrimp in a glass baking dish, and marinate in refrigerator for 1 hour.

Remove shrimp from marinade and place on a greased grill topper. Pour marinade into a small saucepan and heat to a boil. Grill shrimp over hot coals for 4 minutes per side. Brush with garlic sauce while cooking. Spoon any remaining sauce over shrimp and serve.

Serves 4

Brazos Tequila-Lime Grilled Shrimp

1 pound large shrimp, peeled, deveined and butterflied

Marinade:
1 cup olive oil
1/2 cup dry white wine
1/4 cup tequila
2 tablespoons fresh lime juice
2 tablespoons minced garlic
2 tablespoons finely chopped Mexican mint marigold (or tarragon)
2 teaspoons roasted cumin seed, ground or finely crushed
1 teaspoon coriander seed, ground or finely crushed
1/4 teaspoon cayenne pepper
salt and freshly ground pepper to taste
3 tablespoons unsalted butter, chilled

Combine marinade ingredients and pour half over shrimp. Cover and refrigerate overnight, turning occasionally to coat.

Place remaining marinade in a small saucepan over high heat. Cook until liquid is reduced by half. Remove from heat and whisk in chilled butter until sauce thickens. Keep warm, but do not return to a boil. Place shrimp on a greased grill topper and grill over medium coals for about 5 minutes, turning once. Do not overcook. Serve warm with sauce.

Serves 2

This recipe appears courtesy of Nancy Beckham, chef at the Brazos Restaurant in Dallas, Texas.

Whole Snapper with Tarragon Butter

2 (1-3/4–2 pound) red snappers, dressed
2 medium sized bunches fresh dill, coarsely chopped
4 tablespoons vegetable oil

Tarragon Butter:
2 tablespoons white wine vinegar
4 tablespoons dry white wine
1/2 cup (1 stick) unsalted butter, chilled
8–10 fresh tarragon leaves, chopped
Salt and freshly ground pepper to taste

Stuff both red snappers with dill, then carefully tie each fish shut.

To make tarragon butter, combine vinegar and wine over heat and whisk in butter 1 tablespoon at a time. Add tarragon, salt, and pepper. Set aside.

Brush fish with vegetable oil and place on a grill topper. Grill for 10 to 12 minutes, turning once or twice (do not overcook). Fillet fish and serve 1 fillet per person with tarragon butter.

Serves 4

Red Snapper Stir-Grill

1 pound red snapper fillets
2 cups sliced mushrooms
1/2 green bell pepper, julienned
1/2 red bell pepper, julienned
1/2 small onion, julienned

Marinade:
1 tablespoon curry powder
1/2 teaspoon ground coriander
1/4 teaspoon cumin
1 clove garlic, minced
1 tablespoon vegetable oil
1 tablespoon sesame oil
Juice of 1/2 lemon

Combine marinade ingredients in a glass bowl. Cut fillets into 1-inch cubes and add to marinade. Refrigerate for 30 minutes.

Pour fish cubes into a well-greased grill-wok and add vegetables. Stir-grill over hot coals for 6 to 8 minutes, using wooden spoons for tossing. Close lid on grill and cook for 2 to 4 minutes more. Serve hot.

Serves 4

Pacific Snapper with Chervil Butter

4 (6–8-ounce) Pacific snapper fillets
Juice of 1 lemon
Salt and freshly ground pepper to taste
Olive oil
Lemon slices for garnish
Chervil sprigs for garnish

Chervil Butter:
1/2 cup (1 stick) butter, softened
2 tablespoons chopped fresh chervil
Freshly ground pepper to taste

To prepare butter, combine all ingredients, place mixture on waxed paper, and roll into a log. Refrigerate.

Squeeze lemon juice over each fillet, then sprinkle with salt and pepper. Grill fish over hot coals for 5 minutes per side, basting with olive oil. Serve each fillet with a pat of chervil butter and garnish with a chervil sprig atop a lemon slice.

Serves 4

Stir-Grilled Swordfish

4 swordfish fillets, cubed
1/4 pound snow peas, stemmed
1/4 pound shiitake mushrooms
1 (8-ounce) can sliced water chestnuts, drained

Marinade:
1/2 cup soy sauce
1/2 cup dry cooking sherry
1 tablespoon lemon juice
1/4 cup vegetable oil
2 cloves garlic, crushed

Combine marinade ingredients and pour over fish and vegetables in a shallow glass bowl. Refrigerate for about 2 hours.

Place fish and vegetables in a grill wok and drain over sink. Stir-grill over hot coals for 8 to 10 minutes, tossing several times while cooking. Serve immediately.

Serves 6

Bilbo's Swordfish with Pineapple Salsa

6 (7–8-ounce) swordfish fillets
Salt and freshly ground white pepper to taste
1-1/2–2 tablespoons olive oil
3 lemons, quartered

Pineapple Salsa:
1 fresh pineapple, cored, peeled, and quartered
1/2 cup diced red bell pepper
1/2 cup diced green bell pepper
1/4 cup finely chopped red onion
2 tablespoons vegetable oil
2 tablespoons finely chopped cilantro
1 tablespoon fresh lime juice
1 teaspoon chives
1 tablespoon finely chopped fresh parsley
2 teaspoons minced Serrano chili
1/2 teaspoon salt
1/2 teaspoon pepper

To prepare salsa, place pineapple on a baking sheet and broil until fruit just begins to brown (about 5 minutes per side). Chop into 1/4-inch cubes and place in a large bowl. Mix in next 9 ingredients, and then sprinkle with salt and pepper. Cover and refrigerate for 2 hours.

Lay fillets on a clean surface and squeeze 1 lemon wedge over each. Lightly season each fillet with salt and white pepper, then brush lightly with olive oil. Swordfish may be grilled (6 to 10 minutes), broiled (9 to 12 minutes), or sauteed (8 to 11 minutes), though grilled is best. Do not overcook.

To serve, place each fillet in a pool of salsa and garnish with remaining lemon wedges.

Serves 6

This recipe appears courtesy of Captain Bilbo's restaurant in Memphis, Tennessee.

Swordfish Kabobs

2 (12–14-ounce) swordfish steaks or fillets

Barbecue Sauce:
1/2 cup salad oil
1/4 cup lemon juice
1 cup water
1 cup chili sauce
1/4 cup steak sauce
1 tablespoon cider vinegar
1/4 green bell pepper, chopped
2 tablespoons onion, chopped
1 clove garlic, chopped
1-1/2 teaspoons sugar
1 teaspoon paprika
1 teaspoon salt
1/2 teaspoon dry mustard
1/2 teaspoon dry ginger
Dash of cayenne pepper

Combine sauce ingredients in a saucepan and simmer for 1 hour. (Extra sauce will keep in refrigerator for 10 to 12 days.)

Cube fish and thread on skewers. Grill over hot coals for 10 minutes, basting with sauce and turning skewers often. Serve with additional sauce on the side.

Serves 4

Grilled Tilapia and Cucumber Sticks

4 (6-ounce) tilapia fillets
1/2 cup Italian dressing
2 teaspoons balsamic vinegar

Soak a handful (about 1 cup) of mesquite chips in water for several hours. Place fillets in a glass dish. Combine dressing and vinegar, pour over fish, and marinate for 20 to 30 minutes. Reserve marinade for basting.

Throw soaked mesquite chips on hot coals a few minutes before grilling. Place fish on a greased grill topper and grill over hot coals for 4 to 5 minutes per side. Baste with reserved marinade while grilling. Serve with **Cucumber Sticks**.

Serves 4

Cucumber Sticks

2 cucumbers
1 tablespoon rice wine vinegar
1 tablespoon soy sauce
1 teaspoon sugar

Peel, halve lengthwise, and seed cucumbers. Cut into thin, 2-inch sticks. Refrigerate in a covered bowl for several hours or overnight. Drain off liquid and add vinegar, soy sauce, and sugar. Chill thoroughly and toss well before serving.

Serves 4

Trout with Lemon Zest Baste

2 whole rainbow trout, dressed
1 lemon, sliced
1/2 small onion, sliced
Salt and freshly ground pepper to taste

Lemon Zest Baste:
4 tablespoons butter
Juice of 1 lemon
Zest of 1 lemon

To prepare baste, melt butter in a small saucepan, then add lemon juice and zest. Set aside.

Place 2 or 3 lemon and onion slices in the cavity of each fish and season with salt and pepper. Reserve remaining lemon slices.

Grill trout over hot coals for 6 to 7 minutes per side or until meat turns white and flakes easily. Brush with lemon baste often during grilling. Serve garnished with lemon slices.

Serves 2

Cilantro-Buttered Trout
with Tomato Salsa

4 whole rainbow trout, dressed
2 lemons, sliced
4 sprigs cilantro plus 1 tablespoon chopped
Salt and freshly ground pepper to taste
1/2 cup (1 stick) butter
2 tablespoons lemon juice
Cooked brown rice

Tomato Salsa:
2 cups chopped ripe tomatoes
1/2 onion, diced
3 banana peppers, diced
1/4 cup Italian dressing
1/4 teaspoon red pepper flakes

Combine all salsa ingredients and refrigerate.

Place 2 or 3 slices of lemon and 1 sprig of cilantro in the cavity of each fish. Season with salt and pepper.

Melt butter and add lemon juice plus 1 tablespoon of chopped cilantro. Set aside.

Grill trout over hot coals for 6 to 7 minutes per side until meat turns white, basting occasionally with cilantro-butter mixture. Serve with tomato salsa and brown rice.

Serves 4

Pepper Tuna

4 (6–8-ounce) tuna steaks
4 tablespoons pink peppercorns
4 tablespoons green peppercorns
1 lemon, cut into wedges

Crush together pink and green peppercorns and use to coat surface of each steak. Grill fish over hot coals for approximately 2-1/2 minutes per side. (Notice the short cooking time; tuna will toughen if overcooked.) Serve with lemon wedges.

Serves 4

This recipe appears courtesy of Brenda Burns, chef-owner of Californos restaurant in Kansas City, Missouri.

Grilled Tuna Steak with Nectarine–Red Onion Relish

4 (8–10-ounce) boneless tuna steaks, 1-inch thick
4 tablespoons salad oil
Salt and freshly ground white pepper to taste

Nectarine–Red Onion Relish:
1 red bell pepper, seeded and julienned
6 ripe but firm nectarines, peeled and cut into 8 slices
   each
1 medium red onion, julienned
1 teaspoon minced garlic
1/4 cup julienned fresh basil
1/4 cup red wine vinegar
1/4 cup fresh orange juice
2 tablespoons lime juice (about 1 lime)
1/4 cup virgin olive oil
Salt and freshly cracked pepper to taste

Combine all relish ingredients in a large bowl and toss gently.
Mixture will be slightly runny. Chill until ready to serve.
Lightly rub tuna steaks with oil and season with salt and pepper. Grill for 4 to 5 minutes per side over a medium-hot fire
(do not overcook). Check for doneness by bending a steak
gently and looking inside for a slight translucence in the center. Remove from the grill and serve on top of a pool of relish.

Serves 4

*This recipe appears courtesy of Chris Schlesinger, Ph.B.,
coauthor of The Thrill of the Grill. Chris suggests substituting
peaches or plums for the nectarines as a recipe variation.*

Whitefish and Three-Pepper Stir-Grill

1 pound whitefish fillets
1 red bell pepper, julienned
1 green bell pepper, julienned
1 yellow bell pepper, julienned
1 tomato, seeded and julienned
1/2 onion, julienned

Marinade:
1/3 cup olive oil
2 tablespoons white wine vinegar
Juice of 1 lemon
2 tablespoons chopped fresh thyme
2 tablespoons chopped fresh basil
3 cloves garlic, minced
Salt and freshly ground pepper to taste

Combine marinade ingredients in a large glass bowl or resealable plastic bag. Cut fillets into 1-1/2-inch cubes and add to marinade along with vegetables. Marinate in refrigerator for 30 minutes.

Pour mixture into a greased grill wok over sink to partially drain. Stir-grill over hot coals for 6 to 8 minutes, tossing with wooden spoons. Move to indirect-heat side of grill and close lid over grill. Cook for 2 to 4 minutes more. Serve immediately.

Serves 4

This is another "show stopper" stir-grill recipe. Add a salad and it's a meal.

Grilled Whitefish with Strawberry Salsa

4 (6–8 ounce) whitefish fillets or steak
6 tablespoons butter or margarine
1 teaspoon Dijon mustard

Strawberry Salsa:
2 cups chopped ripe strawberries
2 tablespoons chopped fresh mint
2 tablespoons sugar
2 tablespoons dark rum

Combine salsa ingredients in a small bowl and set aside.

Melt butter in a small saucepan and blend in mustard. Baste 1 side of fillets or steak and place basted-side down on a medium-hot grill. Baste while cooking and grill for 4 to 5 minutes per side. Serve with salsa on the side.

Serves 4

Grilled Yellowtail with Water Chestnut–Scallion Relish

4 (8–10-ounce) yellowtail fillets
4 tablespoons vegetable oil
Salt and freshly cracked pepper to taste

Water Chestnut–Scallion Relish:
1 cup canned water chestnuts, sliced
1-1/2 cups very thinly sliced scallion (tops included)
1 tablespoon sugar
2 tablespoons toasted sesame seeds
3 tablespoons soy sauce
2 tablespoons sesame oil
3 tablespoons rice wine vinegar

To prepare relish, combine water chestnuts and scallions. Add sugar and sesame seeds and toss well. Add soy sauce, sesame oil, and vinegar, and toss again. Serve at once.

Rub fillets with vegetable oil, salt, and pepper. Grill over medium heat, skin-side up, until top surface of fish has a light golden crust (5 to 7 minutes). Flip to skin-side down and grill for 5 to 7 minutes more (do not overcook). Serve accompanied by water chestnut-scallion relish.

Serves 4

This recipe appears courtesy of Chris Schlesinger, Ph.B., coauthor of The Thrill of the Grill. *Chris says not to confuse yellowtail with yellowfin tuna: "Yellowtail is a mild-tasting, large-flaked fish with a firm texture that makes it a natural for grilling."*

Amaretto-Basted Walleye

4 (6–8-ounce) walleye pike fillets
1/2 cup (1 stick) butter or margarine
2 tablespoons sliced almonds
2 tablespoons Amaretto

Saute almonds in butter until lightly browned. Add Amaretto.

Place fillets on a greased grill topper. Grill over hot coals for 4 to 5 minutes per side. Baste with butter mixture while cooking. To serve, place fillets on plates and spoon remaining almond butter over each.

Serves 4

INDEX

Salsas *See also* **Relishes**
Avocado-Corn Salsa, 22
Cantaloupe Salsa, 50
Island Salsa, 44
Pineapple Salsa, 74
Strawberry Salsa, 83
Tomato Salsa, 79
Roasted Red Pepper and Corn Salsa, 20

Sauces
Barbecue Sauce, 76
Caper-Parsley Sauce, 32
Cucumber Sauce, 18
Dilled Cucumber Sauce, 35
Garlic Sauce, 68
Horseradish Sauce, 18
Kiwi Sauce, 42
Mustard Dill Sauce, 56
Pesto Sauce, 24
Satay Sauce, 67
Sherried Mustard Sauce, 66
Tangy Seafood Sauce, 30
Tartar Sauce, 17

Scallops
Seafood Skewers, 61
Stir-Grilled Scallops, 60
Sea Bass with Pesto Sauce, 24
Seafood Skewers, 61

Shark
Balsamic Grilled Shark, 63
Mako Shark with Cilantro-Lime Butter, 62

Shrimp *See also* **Prawns**
Brazos Tequila-Lime Grilled Shrimp, 69
Grilled Shrimp Scampi with Garlic Sauce, 68
Lemon-Basil Basted Shrimp, 64
Shrimp on a Stick with Sherried Mustard Sauce, 66

Side Dishes
Aunt Laretta's Slaw, 29
Cucumber Sticks, 77
Grilled Garden Onions, 46

HOOKED ON BOOKS ON GRILLING AND BARBECUING

BARBECUE GREATS MEMPHIS STYLE by Carolyn Wells (1989, Pig Out Publications, Inc.)

BARBECUE: SIZZLING FIRESIDE KNOW-HOW by Leslie Bloom (1987, American Cooking Guild)

BAR-B-QUE, BARBECUE, BARBEQUE, BAR-B-Q, B-B-Q by Carolyn Wells (1991, Pig Out Publications, Inc.)

GRILL LOVER'S COOKBOOK (1985, from Char-Broil, Columbus, GA)

JAMES McNAIR'S GRILL COOKBOOK by James McNair (1990, Chronicle Books)

THE JOY OF GRILLING by Joe Famularo (1988, Barron's)

KANSAS CITY BBQ—THE HOW TO AND WHERE TO OF KANSAS CITY BARBECUE by Rick Welch and Bill Venable (1989, Pig Out Publications, Inc.)

KANSAS CITY BBQ POCKETGUIDE by Remus Powers, Ph.B. (1992, Pig Out Publications, Inc.)

THE PASSION OF BARBEQUE by The Kansas City Barbeque Society (1992, Hyperion)

THE THRILL OF THE GRILL by Chris Schlesinger and John Willoughby (1990, William Morrow and Company)

ABOUT THE AUTHORS

Karen Adler is president of Pig Out Publications, Inc., a publishing company that specializes in barbecue and grilling books. She coauthored *Kansas City Cuisine* with Shifra Stein and has published numerous regional food and travel books. She is a founding charter member of the Kansas City chapter of the American Institute of Wine and Food. Karen is a recent graduate of the Greasehouse University and received the distinguished M.B. (Master of Barbecue) degree. When Karen is not at the publishing office, you may find her in the kitchen or at the grill cooking for friends and family.

Rick Welch is a barbecue zealot, a cofounder of the Kansas City Barbeque Society (KCBS), and coauthor of *Kansas City BBQ: The How To and Where To of Kansas City Barbecue.* Barbecue is his life—not only his avocation but his vocation as well. Rick is a partner in Pig Out Publications, Inc. and owner of River City Products. His company specializes in the manufacturing of barbecue spices and marinades, making barbecue a 24-hour concern! Rick is also a charter member of the Kansas City chapter of the American Institute of Wine and Food.

Carolyn Wells loves fish cooked on the grill. She, too, is a cofounder of the Kansas City Barbeque Society and publishes its newsletter, "The Bullsheet." Carolyn has won over 150 awards in barbecue contests. Through that love of barbecue and the countless hours spent grillside, she has developed into an accomplished and innovative grill master. She is a member of the KCBS "Hall of Flame" and has earned her Ph.B. (Doctor of Barbecue Philosophy). She is the author of *Barbecue Greats Memphis Style* and *Barbecue, Barbeque, Bar-B-Q, B-B-Q* and a partner in Pig Out Publications, Inc. Carolyn is a founding charter member of the Kansas City chapter of the American Institute of Wine and Food.

PIG OUT PUBLICATIONS, INC. ORDER FORM

ORDER DIRECT--CALL (816) 842-8880

YES! I want to order a barbecue cookbook(s) so I can start cooking like the pros. Please send me:

—— copy/copies of **Barbecue Greats Memphis Style** for $12.95 plus $2 shipping.

—— copy/copies **The Passion of Barbeque** for $9.95 plus $2 shipping .

—— copy/copies **Hooked on Fish on the Grill** for $8.95 plus $2 shipping.

—— copy/copies **Bar-B-Que, Barbecue, Barbeque, Bar-B-Q, B-B-Q** for $5.95 plus $2 shipping.

—— copy/copies **Kansas City BBQ Pocketguide** for $7.95 plus $2 shipping.

METHOD OF PAYMENT:

—— Enclosed is my check for $ ——
(payable to PIG OUT PUBLICATIONS, INC.)
Please charge to my credit card: ——VISA ——Mastercard

Account #_____

Signature _____

SHIP TO: _____   **Gift/ship to:** _____

_____   _____

_____   _____

_____   **From:** _____

MAIL COMPLETED ORDER FORM TO:

Pig Out Publications, Inc. 4245 Walnut Kansas City, MO 64111